SUCCESS

IN 3D

Three Laws of Success

Kelvin Easter

True Potential
REACH THE WORLD

Success in 3D
Three Laws of Success

Cover and interior page design by True Potential, Inc.

ISBN: 9781948794831 (paperback)
ISBN: 9781948794848 (ebook)

True Potential
REACH THE WORLD

True Potential, Inc.
PO Box 904, Travelers Rest, SC 29690
www.truepotentialmedia.com

Produced and Printed in the United States of America.

Acknowledgment

This book was written but not published before the untimely passing of my mother, Loretta Easter.

Mom, you were able to read the unpublished pages of this book. Finally, it is now going to be published.

Mom, you are an incredible gift, you are the greatest of all time. I love you immensely! There is NOT a day that has gone by where I haven't thought about you several times and heard your voice. I look forward to being reunited with you when I am finished with my assignment on the earth. I am at peace because you are happier than you ever have been while managing life on earth. All I am I owe to you and dad. You lived a selfless life so that Dad, Darnell and I could blossom. You are being rewarded for your selfless stewardship in many ways now. I love you forever!

Dedication

This book is dedicated to the most intimate of all my incredible relationships.

To my dad, Jimmy D. Easter; What a man, what a gift, what a general, what a special person you are. I am today a man of resilience because of you. I am a man of God because of you. I talk with you almost every day, a couple of times a day. Dad, you are my hero. All you and mom sacrificed to make our pathway easier will never be forgotten. I love you, dad. This book would not have been possible without your love, care and nurture throughout the years. You are an incredible example of love, integrity, and consistency. I love you immensely. Thank you for everything. Thank you for believing in Darnell and me.

To my brother and sister-in-law, James and Cherryl Easter: During some of the most difficult times in my life, you have demonstrated tremendous love and stability, with the voice of Godly reasoning. You have helped to anchor me and are divinely sent from God to assist in my formation. I love you both.

To my spiritual father who birthed me, with confidence, into the ministry, Bishop C. L Easter: Your example and work ethic as my pastor and mentor have had an indelible influence on my ministry. Thank you for being faithful. You have made a positive impact on many lives. I love and appreciate you, sir.

To my Spiritual father, in revelation, the late Pastor James E. Watson: I sincerely miss our intimate, biblical conversations and cherish the years of fellowship, mentoring and development under your ministry. I have truly received the impartation. Your words are coming to pass as I follow the path you made, as a father, in biblical revelation. I am carrying on the torch and look forward to our talks, in glory.

To my heart physics coach, mentor, and friend, Dr. James B. Richards: Your incredible wisdom, knowledge, and revelation of grace and of the intricacies of the heart, have taken my life and ministry to another level. I count our time together as priceless. Thank you for being you.

To Prophet/Pastor John Veal. John your consistent encouragement over the past year and a half to get my intellectual work published has been huge. You are an incredible gift to me, the Destined to Win Christian Center and the body of Christ at large. Continue to minister as you do with integrity and travel the world. I am humbled to join you on the authors journey.

To my two awesome children, Chanel and Isaiah Easter: I am so proud of you. You have done well and have been a delight. The two of you have made us proud. I am crazy about you both and look forward to what God has for your future, *the very best is yours if you continue to follow God's path. I love you, with a love I can't describe. Remember, my ceiling is to be your floor.*

To my three nephews Stephen and Joshua Easter, Cortez Martin and Andre Nelson Jr: I am extremely proud of the men you have become. I am truly blessed to have you in my life.

To my nieces Candace Adley and Christine Jon'el: Remember all we have taught you. Give your love and life to Christ. You are loved and appreciated more than you know. To all of you, my ceiling should also be your floor.

To my mother in law, Myrtle Blue: I have never had a cross word with you, in over 30 years. You have always treated me as a son. I love you, mom. Thanks for birthing Tonya.

To my father in law James T. Blue: I appreciate our conversations and the love and support you have shown me throughout the years. I respect and love you.

To my sisters-in-law, LaShawn and Cheree and brothers-in-law Martice and Ted: What a blessing it is to have your love, in my life. I am truly blessed by your support and friendship.

To my most prized and beloved, Tonya Denise Easter: You have been an incredible wife. I celebrate the beauty in you and have been overwhelmingly blessed by our life together. It has been a delight to see you grow in your gifts, callings, and talents. You are an outstanding mother to our children. You are the first and ONLY lady. You are the strength of my life outside of the Lord and are a blessing to our congregation.

Due to your uncomplicated support, I continue to grow in my life, ministry and business endeavors and I am unrestricted in my commitment to the Lord's call. If I had to do it all over again. I would marry you again. I love you with all my heart. Thank you!

To the Destined to Win Christian Center family: Your loyalty and honor is evident. The best is yet to come. My earnest desire is to see your life change, from glory to glory.

To my Lord and Savior Jesus Christ: You are the reason I exist. You are the hope, light, and love of my life. Thank you, for choosing me before I chose you and for liberating my heart from the bondage of religion. I now bask in the sweetness of your grace. Thank you for calling me into your ministry at the age of 17 and for keeping my heart pure, through your correction. May you live through me, for the rest of my life on this earth, making an incredible impact on the lives of many. May I live as a man of character and continue to die to myself, that you may live abundantly. May I serve others as you have modeled for me.

Contents

Introduction

Success in 3D is the result of over 25 years of personal development and leadership experience. My passion is to see people of all groups, win in life. Over the years, I have been intentionally committed to my personal growth. I have invested thousands of dollars toward the development of my personal life and leadership skills. I believe the Creator designed us to maximize our potential in the spiritual, mental and physical realms, of our lives.

We are to be holistic in our growth and development. I have experienced great results, through the application of God's laws and principles, which govern life, on our planet. I hope you will become as passionate as I am, about growing and winning in life. Success in 3D covers three incredible laws, which I feel are key to personal achievement. A law is a statement of fact, deduced from observation to the effect that a particular natural or scientific phenomenon always occurs if certain conditions are present.

Over the years, I have observed and studied the laws of Desire, Discovery, and Discipline and have found them to be integral to the achievements of mankind; without respect of person, race or religion. I truly believe these attributes are essential to success in life. Therefore, I have chosen to call them laws in this writing. Now, for the record, this treatment is, by no means, an exhaustive study of these laws. Neither was it intended to be an exegete on an exclusively biblical basis or any passage of scripture, from the ancient text. Rather, my intentions are for it to serve as a catalyst for spurring thought. It is written to challenge the mind and to encourage the reader to study how things work. It is meant to stimulate curiosity in the seeker's heart, toward discovering truth.

I would like to encourage you, as you begin reading this book, to prepare your heart and set your intention for maximum benefit. Take good notes and use a highlighter. Remember, repetition is the mother of learning. You will not get all you can, from the first reading. Activate the law of repetition by reviewing this book and your notes often. Over the years, I have committed myself to the practice of repetition and have reaped the benefits. Now, activate your mind and heart with the intention of ascending to a higher level.

CHAPTER 1

The Power of Desire

Desire is one of the greatest qualities of the human heart. I believe the employment and activation of desire, is one of the master keys, to success in life. The Bible says, *"Whatsoever things you desire when you pray, believe that you will receive them, and you will have them."* (Mark 11:24) I have heard many teachings and commentaries on this statement, but never with the emphasis on desire. I submit to you, that the most potent part of this statement is the phrase, "Whatsoever you DESIRE."

In the human experience and throughout nature, the supreme catalyst for results comes down to this question: "How badly do you want it?" Let me explain. The base nature in all of creation is the quality of desire. Your eyes desire to see, your ears desire to hear, your nose desires to smell, etc. There is nothing in your life or in nature that does not want. Words that are synonymous with desire include: to long for, crave, covet, thirst, hunger, want, wish, and to yearn for. Desire is neutral in the human heart and will work for or against you. Your desires can serve the virtues or vices of life, creating good habits or bad habits. Desire can be the catalyst for good or for evil.

Since my teenage years, I have had a determination in my heart, to be successful in all my endeavors. In 1982, I employed, merely by accident, fixed universal laws that were designed by God to give me the edge I needed, to succeed in high school. I did not understand these laws prior to this time, but today I understand firsthand, the power of desire.

Desire Awakened

It was the beginning of my junior year of high school and my parents and I were on our way to my final class review, at the annual fall parent/teachers, conference night. This event was designed for the instructors and parents to review the student's progress for the quarter. Up until this point, I had gotten away with really weak performances in most of my classes but was still passing. To be honest with you, at the time, I knew I was just getting by but was willing to accept mediocrity.

Let me put this scene into perspective for you. It was our final class visit of the evening. This visit was with my physics teacher, Mr. Robert Hetzel. Two cousins and my brother James had preceded me, in attending Mr. Hetzel's class. Each of them had done very well academically. James had graduated in the prior year. This was to become a night to remember.

Updating Mr. Hetzel on my brother's activities and

achievements served as an icebreaker. James was an honor student and was in his first year at the University of Illinois at Champaign Urbana, in the engineering program. To be crystal clear, I was never jealous of my brother; in fact, it was an honor to be his younger brother. I looked up to him and was proud of his accomplishments.

So, they were talking and laughing about James, while I was personally interested in getting the conference over with. Finally, he began to discuss my progress. It started well, with a compliment on my attendance, and then suddenly, things went south. I will never forget his words, as long as I live. He said, "Kelvin has a D- average on his quizzes, a D- average on his exams, and he has turned in five of fifteen homework assignments. These are the reasons he received a failing grade in his coursebook.

It started well, with a compliment on my attendance, and then suddenly, things went south.

Now call me dumb, stupid or just plain naïve, because I was not expecting to fail this class. I was completely shocked. I felt as though someone had slapped me across my face with a wet rag. I was devastated. I did not hear another word spoken. I slowly left the classroom, then began to walk quickly down the hallway. Suddenly a friend of mine began to yell my name, asking how I had done. Now, as you might imagine, I had no interest in talking to anyone. I had just gotten an "F" bomb dropped on me!

I jogged out of the building and made a mad dash to my parent's car. With tears in my eyes and disappointment in my heart, I leaned on the car, contemplating my failure. I dreaded having to discuss my results with my parents. Now don't get me wrong, my parents were the most compassionate, caring parents a teenager could have. They always tried to motivate me to do my best, but that was precisely the reason I didn't want to talk to them. They had done all they could for me. I felt like I had failed them as well as myself.

Finally, my parents arrived. Neither of them said anything at the beginning of the drive home. I broke the silence. I shared my disappointment with them and like usual, they did their best to encourage me. At the time, I began to recall, several similar discussions over the preceding year and a half. This time was different. When the instructor delivered the bad news, something changed inside my heart. This experience was a significant, defining moment in my life. You see, I had become so disgusted, angry, disappointed and fed up, that I'd activated my hunger for change.

My desire to change for the better would not be denied.

The sleeping giant of desire was now awakened. My desire to change for the better would not be denied. It is amazing how the laws that govern success, arise, attract and cleave to the determined heart. I never wanted to experience that kind of disappointment again. Instead of blaming others or making excuses, my mind went into overdrive, to resolve this challenge. Right there in the automobile, without paper and pen, I self-assessed, devised and formulated a complete plan of action.

The next few days were full of change. My strong desire gave rise to me becoming more organized. I used all the facts and knowledge I'd known, about what it took to become an academic success. I was determined to implement new habits, necessary for educational success. I was intent on activating, what I now know as, the law of sacrifice. I was willing to pay every necessary price. I instituted parameters on my social life and my attitude toward academics. I also implemented structure and objectives to guide my study habits, which would enable me to obtain my desired goal. God, my parents, and my instructors would all report I had gone through a complete and immediate transformation.

By activating my desire and intensifying my hunger for change, I received all the wisdom necessary to change my future. I am a living example of this true saying, "When the student is ready the teacher will appear." I earned a "B" the next quarter of my physics class and had worked diligently to achieve a "B" average in the rest of my classes. Seeing how successful I was becoming, I set my goals even higher. I aspired for straight "As" in every class for the remainder of my high school career. Mission accomplished! I averaged a 4.0 for the next year and a half.

The rest is history. I would never look back. I knew inside my heart, that I really could do almost anything if I truly wanted it bad enough. I would never again be denied because I had discovered a universal truth. Let me take a minute to encourage any teenagers that are reading this. I was sixteen years old when this change occurred in my life. I was a "D- "student and became a straight "A" student. That was over 35 years ago. I want you to understand that you can excel and be victorious in school. You just have to begin with the desire to want to be better, to do better and to excel, then put a plan into action. My organization is committed to assisting young people in unleashing their potential through our mentoring and coaching program. I believe one generation's ceiling should be the next generation's floor.

CHAPTER 2

The Law of Desire

Desire is the unseen force that serves as the catalyst for all great achievements. The real problem with most people is that they are lackluster, lazy and lukewarm in their desire. You see, God created absolute laws that govern the way life works. The trigger for the manifestation of these laws is your desire. You have to WANT, bad enough! You have to go to bed and get up every morning, driven with an inward determination to win!

We have all seen this law in operation, in every arena of life. When desire is activated in overdrive, incredible things happen. The unique thing about this wisdom principle is that once it is intimately established in your heart, no one can take it away from you. It becomes a part of your life forever. I excelled in every position I held in the corporate world. This was no easy feat, considering it was within a direct consumer sales organization. I achieved success as an independent contractor, recruiter, an assistant manager and as a senior-level director. The knowledge and activation of this one principle made me a top award winner for 7 years and enabled me to earn a six-figure income in the business world.

Today, I am living my 30-year dream to develop effective leaders and to help people win in life. It was this unyielding desire to inspire positive life change that helped me to realize this dream.

Most people never realize their dreams, because they don't want it bad enough!

I want you to clearly understand, desire alone does not create success. Desire is the catalyst. It is the fuel needed to activate another law: The Law of Discovery. The Law of Discovery, which we will discuss next, is summed up in a famous quote from the Word of God, "Seek and you shall find, knock and the door shall be opened, ask and it shall be given." (Matthew 7:7) Notice, there are three absolute outcomes to each segment of that quote. Nothing in life has to be forced into operation.

You have to go to bed and get up every morning driven with an inward determination to win.

Success in life is much simpler than most of us think. In fact, all that you can potentially be and do in life is already present; it does not need to be forced into manifestation. It has to be discovered. Everything you need, all the resources necessary to fulfill your God-given dreams, is already available. You can be a person of character, a great leader, a great spouse, a great parent and a loyal friend. You can make your mark on this earth, at this time. It is all accessible. You simply must discover it. Discovery does not come without its challenges. This is why your desire must be robust, strong and unyielding, because it is the fuel that enables you to keep seeking, knocking and asking. Without it, we

Most people never realize their dreams because they do not want it bad enough!

cave in, quit and go to the grave rich with treasures that have never been manifested.

The Law of Discovery and the Law of Application will propel you toward your desired outcome. This is a life long journey that will make you an overnight success.

Before we delve into that, let's take some time to talk a little more about the Law of Desire. Desire is the fuel that will give you the winning edge. As stated earlier, desire is neutral; it can be a catalyst for good or for evil. I, of course, am discussing the need to harness and feed desire, to direct it down the avenues which will benefit humanity.

I believe we have a moral obligation to add value to the human experience. Every gift and God-given desire that has ever been born in the heart of the human soul has, in its DNA, an assignment to add value to people. So, regardless of what your dreams consist of, you need to have a tremendous desire to continue to grow personally. This equips you to add value to people's lives, as you walk toward your destiny.

Inherent in all of God's creation, is this law of desire. Desire is the first property of all nature. As I stated earlier, your ears desire to hear, your eyes desire to see, your nose desires to smell, your heart desires to pump, the blood in your body desires to flow, your tongue desires to taste. This desire is a fire; it can develop into an inferno, which sets the heart ablaze with possibilities. It is the fuel that is seen in the incredible accomplishments of athletes like Michael Jordan, LeBron James, Tiger Woods, and Serena Williams. It also ignited the talents of entertainers like Sylvester Stallone, Dustin Hoffman, Denzel Washington, Michael Jackson, and Oprah Winfrey. It is the foundation for a remarkable work ethic and persistence. Indomitable desire is also responsible for motivating us to get back up when we fail. This desire will not allow you to stay down. It will talk you back into the game. Desire is the foundation for life's great achievements. It has an insatiable appetite and can grow strong in your life, but you must feed it.

> All that you can potentially be and do in life is present; it does not need to be forced into manifestation. It has to be discovered!

Now, it has been said, that you can do anything you want to do if you want it badly enough. This is only true, within the proper context. That context is within the realm of your gift, talent mix, and personal design. Therefore, it is imperative that you employ the Laws of Discovery to unveil your gifts, talents and your personal design. When it comes to learning and growing in wisdom; barring a major disability, I believe everyone's mind can expand

and grow to obtain wisdom to achieve. I truly believe all of us have a type of genius in our hearts. We were all born to add value and to do great things. We all have the potential for unlimited expression, because the source of our existence, through our creator, is unlimited. A definite purpose, mission or aim is paramount.

You have to know what you want. I've shared with you when this law of desire was awakened in my heart. My definite aim and purpose were to become an academic success. I was so fed up and disgusted that I resolved to change. I was no longer satisfied with mediocrity and failure. Now, of course, several things will happen when you determine what you really want. Notice first, your inner image changes. You imagine a different version of yourself and can actually see it in your mind's eye. In other words, we change inside before we change outside. This bears repeating: You and I change on the inside before there is visible, noticeable change on the outside.

A well-known piece of wisdom states, "The solutions to your problems are not found at the same level of thought in which they were created." You have to go up to another level and see out of a different window to overcome certain problems and obstacles. This is what I call being solution minded. Understand this, desire can be as powerful as an assassin. If it is properly fed and unleashed it can kill every excuse and paralyze all doubt standing in your path to discovery.

We all have the ability to be where we are going before we actually arrive, through the power of our imagination. It's desire that activates imagination. So, as we begin to see and understand, many times, one law will activate another law. Laws and principles often act in tandem with one another. When desire is awakened, everything in the heart and the programmed intelligence in the earth, begin to align, to assist in fulfilling the desired goal. I believe the author of this intelligence is God. He has released laws that have no respect of persons; they are either working for or against you.

We change inside before we change outside

You must be certain of your wants. The laws created, are absolute and programmed to operate via definite commands. Creation identifies only with what you absolutely want and will then begin to make it materialize. Hence the following quote from the Word of God, "A double-minded man is unstable in all of his ways and let this man not think he will receive anything he desires." (James 1:8)

Why? First of all, I believe the great creator is involved in everyone's life and does answer prayer. I have studied and have observed the way life works and it appears that God has programmed intelligence in the earth, that responds to absolutes. It also appears that the universe cannot and will not process confused and unstable commands. There must be clear, definite requests or decrees that are truly desired in the heart, not in the mind alone.

The truth herein is that laws govern everything occurring in the universe and on planet earth. After I became clear regarding what I wanted and defined my intentions, the intelligence in the earth, designed by God, worked with me as a servant. It assisted me in achieving straight A's and in accomplishing high achievements, in other areas of my life. But there are other aspects to life that are a science such as the Law of Cause and Effect or Sowing and Reaping, the Law of Desire and hundreds more. The Law of Desire is a science that will work for or against you every time it is employed. It is a law that will not be denied.

There are three common ways we can influence our desires:

1. Through observation- That is what we see through our eye gates

2. Through associations – This deals with who and what we are exposed to and who we associate with.

3. Through teachings: What we have been taught and are being taught.

These three areas have the power to influence and feed our desire to cause it to grow. That's the reason why we will go no further than the people we associate with and the information we are exposed to. You must place yourself in a fertile environment in order to expand, to grow and to move forward. It's crucial that we understand the essential place desire has in being a catalyst to everything we want to achieve in life. Desire is lying dormant in so many

Desire can be as powerful as an assassin. If it is continually fed and unleashed it can kill every excuse and paralyze all doubt standing in your path to discovery.

people, but God wants us to release desire. He wants us to build, grow and feed it so that it can mature and assist in taking us to a higher level.

Now, whether you realize it or not, every day of your life, your desires are being influenced by what you have observed, who you associate with, and what you have been taught. The eye and the ear gates are the bridge to the heart. Desire is a quality of the heart. Because this is true, it is important to intentionally do what you can to correctly influence your desires. Desire is common to all mankind.

Here's an example I use to illustrate how deep and potent desire is: If I literally dropped you off in the desert with a bottle of water and a container of urine or motor oil, as long as you have water you would never think about drinking either the urine or the motor oil. But let's say you run out of the water and you are days away from a refill. The thirst and desire for water would be so great that your body would begin to convince your mind that drinking the motor oil or urine would quench your thirst (desire). Eventually, the intensity of your desire would win over common sense. This is an extreme example, but desire of the heart is that strong and potent. It simply needs to be awakened to its potential through a proper environment.

All of us have latent or hidden desire. I don't intend to be overly spiritual, but God didn't create anything without first desiring it. In fact, there is not one thing that is brought into existence in the earth that is not predicated by a man or woman desiring it. Nothing will change or be rearranged, without their first being a strong desire. This is the reason why personal transformation and the fulfillment of your destiny is contingent upon how bad you want it.

Now let's stop for a moment. I have included a self-coaching assessment, which you should complete before moving forward. Please go to a solitary place and take about an hour to think through your responses and complete the assessment. It is important to be brutally honest and transparent in your self-evaluation for it to be effective. If time is an issue at present, schedule an appointment with yourself within the next couple of days, to do so. However, I would suggest you complete the assessment, before continuing to read.

Self-Coaching Assessment

Ask yourself the following questions and conduct a brainstorming session with paper and pen.

- How badly do you want your life to change?

- How badly do you want to be healthy?

- How badly do you want to achieve?

- Be honest…being brutally honest is important!

- Next, ask yourself, "How am I feeding this desire?"

- Am I observing things that feed my desire and help me to see and envision my goal as achieved?

- Who am I associating with?

- When I look at my circle of friends and associates how many have advanced further than me? Can I learn from them?

- Who is teaching me? What am I being taught? Is it feeding my desire?

- What books, audio, and video resources I have planned to intentionally read, listen to and observe?

- Does my checkbook reveal my heart as far as my personal development is concerned?

This is a contemplative exercise that will help you to realize where you are. When you are finished, we will be ready to go a little further in our lesson.

CHAPTER 3

Growing Desire

Now that you have completed your self-assessment, are you willing to do the work that will enable you to enhance your desire? The unmasking of self-truths can be eye-opening, exciting and yet, a little intimidating. Fear not, you can and will move forward. You simply have to make a staunch commitment to work diligently to gain momentum. I know you are ready, and I am ready to assist you.

Desire can grow daily. The key to the growth of your desire is the intentional feeding of it through the activation of repetition and strong intentionality. It is the continual and intentional effort to prepare your heart to receive impartation from one of the three sources mentioned earlier that will make the difference. For ease of memory, let's now refer to these sources with the acronym O.A.T, (observation, associations, and teachings.) The heart of man is an incredible power that is designed to birth what would be understood by the human mind as impossible.

One of the tremendous qualities of the heart of man is desire. The incubator for desire is your thought life. You must meditate and feed your heart with quality nutrients through observation, through your associations, and through teachings. The more you think on these things, the stronger your desire will become. Next, apply what you are receiving to your own life and teach what you've learned to others. Bit by bit, with continual effort, your desire will become a blaze of fire.

Now as we conclude our lesson on the principle of desire, I want you to understand how important it is to know exactly what you want in life and why you must have a burning desire in order to get what you want. Everything in the universe has received an absolute command from the Creator to produce that which is desired without doubt. The earth or the universe will not respond to an unstable request; in other words, instability and confusion concerning what you desire will not be understood; therefore, nothing will produce. So, take your time and be certain. Then, spend time feeding these dreams and goals so that they indeed become burning desires of the heart.

All great things begin with the power of desire.

Remember, your desire is the catalyst for all movement in the earth and the universe. I am a person of faith, so I will take a moment to explain from a spiritual perspective why desire is unlimited and why it is remarkable in its strength. Desire, in the human heart, is unlimited because it was designed by God, Who is limitless. Mankind was created to interface with God. In fact, according to the Word of God, we were made in His likeness. We are as close as you can get to being God, without being God. Understand, because of the way we were created we would never need to be God. We were made so much like Him that as we interface with Him, His desire, His will, and His thoughts would literally flow through us. This would enable us to work in harmony with Him. In order for the will of God to be done on the earth, mankind would have to be able to draw from God, without any limitations. So, since you were created to desire and need God, your desire literally has no end. This is the reason why, when human beings search for fulfillment outside of a relationship with the Creator, they are left empty. Your innate desire is exclusively for God first. This is an incredible truth, which we must recognize. So, make your search for God through Christ become your number one priority. Overall, deep within the heart of all human beings is the desire to know God, to be more, to do more and to express more, in life. As you meditate on the things we have shared in this lesson, I believe you will awaken the sleeping giant of desire within you, to accomplish great things in life. I know personally, that in doing this, your life could potentially, never be the same. All great things start with the power of desire.

CHAPTER 4

The Law of Discovery

Over the years I have spent thousands of dollars of my own money on personal development. I read several books each year and I am plugged into wisdom, daily. People closest to me know I am always pursuing knowledge in a book, through audio or video teaching, or by attending a conference. In all of my studies, I am surprised to find very little focused work on this amazing law. Understanding the Law of Discovery will take tremendous pressure off your life. It will totally change the way you perceive and approach life's challenges.

Mankind is dominated by fear and force. We believe and have been trained in life, to live in fear and to try to make things happen. This is done mainly by force. We all use the phrase," I've got to go and make it happen" or "If it's going to be, it's up to me," etc. Well, I know what we mean by these statements, so it's ok to say these things, as long as we have the proper perspective of how life really works.

Human beings, for the most part, live in fear. This is because we have fallen from our original created state, which is love. In an environment of love, there is peace and tranquility. In this kind of environment, things work effortlessly. This is the way we were designed to live. Since mankind has become his own source for protection and provision, he believes he has to make things happen or else he will go without. This is why men and women always try to dominate each other. We tend to do all we can, in our competitiveness, to beat the next person to the top. Sometimes, we actively use manipulation, which is the abusive selfish activation of influence, to move things and people, to get what we want. There is a better way to live and to produce in life.

To discover, by definition, is to make known or visible; to obtain sight or knowledge of, for the first time; to detect the presence of, to find, to find out. In other words, to discover is to uncover what already exists. Now, this is huge, when it comes to the way our lives unfold and the way we perceive things. It's really interesting to see, all through life, through the book of wisdom, through nature, and through science, that this law is evident. In the Word of God, you will find this statement, *"Ask and it shall be given, seek and you shall find, knock and the door shall be opened."* (Matthew 7:7) Now, this phrase by itself is a huge clue to the way life really works.

The late Stephen Covey wrote, "All things are created twice." Now, this concept was not originated by Covey. It is a concept that is continually implied, in the Word of God. The word used by Covey is "create". However, none of us actually brings anything into existence from nothing, all things already exist, but they exist in a state beyond our viewing. In other words, you can't see the totality of what already exists. This is a really important point because many of us believe there is lack. There is no actual lack. It is impossible to have God our Creator, create the universe with an abundance mentality and still have lack. It's not possible! I know that science and the different intelligences, tell us there are many shortages. They insist upon watching and policing the population, because of what they claim to be a scarcity of resources, but in reality, there is no such thing as lack or shortage. Now, I can imagine the thoughts racing through your mind saying, "What about Africa? What about all the other desolate places across the world?" The reason there are desolate places in the earth, where there appears

> In life, truth is like a puzzle; one piece is connected to another piece.

to be lack, is because mankind's heart is not aligned to work in congruence with the laws God created. We must understand, there is a catalyst to all change and all prosperity. It begins with cooperation between us and God.

It is necessary, that we learn to spend time pondering truth. In life, truth is like a puzzle; one piece is connected to another piece. Eventually, if you stick with truth, a clear picture of what truly exists comes into view. Consider this, all of the things we see today, in the 21st century, existed in its natural state years before it manifested. You may be asking, "Where did it exist?" Well, at the micro-level, it existed unformed, in an invisible state. This invisible state is known as spirit and it is in this realm, where all truth begins.

Science has taught us that all things are in motion, in other words, things are moving. In physics we understand this to be atoms, protons, neutrons, etc. In my opinion, this area of physics is as close as we can get to what is of spiritual substance. The material and laws that allow for natural manifestation are already in existence. If all things exist first in an unseen state, how does mankind begin the process of discovering things? It's very simple; through thought and imagination.

Now notice, the realm of thought and imagination is still hidden from the natural eye, so going back to Stephen Covey's statement, which is also implied in the Word of God, from our vantage point all things are created twice. Here's what is amazing about this. Where did the thought or the idea come from? Well, you can formulate your own conclusions regarding that question, but here is what we can see clearly. All thoughts and ideas that manifest, good or bad, arise from the invisible realm. We do not, in the literal sense, create the thought. We ponder upon it. In other words, we discover it in its raw, natural, unformed state. When a person chooses to meditate and work with the thought, the "how-to" and the "way" is made to produce, in natural form, what already exists. So, in reality, thoughts are things waiting to be discovered but we must act upon them.

CHAPTER 5

Thoughts on the Canvas of Love

From the beginning of time, all laws that govern life have existed. Two thousand years ago we could have had the iPad, the internet, airplanes, etc. You name it, we could have brought it into existence. The only reason these things were not manifested or invented years ago is that they had not been discovered. Remember, earlier I mentioned that life is like a puzzle. Well, one law has to be discovered and worked in conjunction with other laws. This is why it took so long to discover, what we have today. Now as a disclaimer, I am not disrespecting Steve Jobs or Bill Gates, but Microsoft and Apple technologies were not created by these men. These men did not bring these technologies into existence, from nothing. In reality, these men, with the help of others, employed the Law of Discovery. They tirelessly sought, until they discovered what had already existed and they made a fortune.

These men cannot take credit for bringing these awesome technologies into existence, but they do get credit for discovering them in thought first and for fleshing them out in the natural, from what already existed. Take a moment to look around you. Every street sign, every building, every work of art, even the landscape of nature, began as a thought, in a man or woman's mind. The thinking mind and heart are where the first, so-called, creation exists.

Now, you should be able to see where lack comes from. Literally, a barren mind will yield nothing. Lack originates in the mind and heart of man. Every invention and material thing were brought into existence, following the same process. They were first a thought in the imagination. There is a saying, which I mentioned earlier when we were discussing the Laws of Desire: "When the student is ready, the teacher will appear." This is a truth that has been proven over and over again. Understand that seeing completely into the light, is simply becoming aware of what already exists. Therefore, it is the awareness that allows for discovery in the heart.

Let me explain why the Law of Discovery exists on the earth. Man does not live in absolute light. In origin there is no darkness, no shadows, there is absolute light. The earth is a type; it is a shadow of what is to come and what is real. So, wisdom is accessible but is hidden from the naked eye. Man has fallen from absolute light, love, and life. Therefore, all truth has to be sought after and discovered by human beings.

To help you further see life is all about discovery, let's look at some basic examples. Every person on earth has

Thoughts on the Canvas of Love

a talent or gift. Whatever the talent or gift is, it is not made, it is revealed, or discovered. All music is discovered. Basically, a musician or singer will hear in his head and his heart, sounds that already exist. He simply cultivates what he is hearing, in the invisible world, and plays or sings it into manifestation. We discover who we are in God and we discover truth. Science discovers truths and through trial and error, perfect what it has discovered in real life. We can learn a lot from scientists, on how to activate the Laws of Discovery.

One thing we understand about scientists is that they are deep thinkers. They ask questions and continually ruminate on whatever they are attempting to understand. From one experiment to the next, with an open mind, they are thinking and meditating in a diligent effort to connect one piece to the next. This process includes taking notes and employing a continuous review of each aspect of their research. Again, and again, scientists will ask questions; think through laws and principles and imagine possibilities, until they find the exact piece that fits the puzzle. What is interesting is that they are constantly seeking, asking and knocking for more wisdom. This has been the vehicle for man's progress, over the past 2000 years.

Mankind has thought, imagined and discovered his way to create the trappings of our modern society. There have been thousands of ideas, inventions, and discoveries that have been made through the years, through the process of meditation. To meditate is to ponder on, to muse, and to roll over in one's thoughts, over and over again. This is why, in the book of wisdom, human beings are guaranteed success in life through meditation and application.

As I stated earlier, we as human beings, for the most part, live in fear because we have fallen from our created state of love. In an environment of love, there is peace and tranquility. In this kind of environment, things work effortlessly. This is the way we were designed to live. The highest form of living is a life of love. Love is not self-centered and it's always seeking to give. Love is the catalyst to abundance. It inherently manifests abundance towards anything it comes into contact with. There can be no lack because love has to give. If it has to give, it has to have more than enough to give this time, the next time and forever. So, love has contained within itself, a constant multiplication of expression. It is an expression of giving, which cannot be comprehended by the human soul. Now, hopefully, you are beginning to see that the labor and manipulation we often employ will not and can never yield effortless results. The key to effortless manifestation is in thought, imagination and application. This must be cultivated in an environment of love and peace. When we flow in the state of love, love effortlessly and willingly provides the answers to any problem and reveals wisdom without struggle.

One of the things you have probably picked up on by now is the importance of learning to discipline ourselves to think correctly and to pursuing a life of love that adds value to people. This is why, if one is pursuing wealth apart from the desire to distribute love, the pursuit will be fruitless. Most people who become rich, besides receiving an inheritance, did so by discovering something that would add value to or solve a problem for, the human race. Love is the catalyst for abundant effortless living. I can honestly tell you that since I have discovered these truths, my life has been enriched far beyond what I initially thought I would experience. This is the reason you and I never need to know how to do anything. When we step up to the line of intentionality armed with love and our "why," we will discover the "how."

The law of discovery is very powerful. I believe, as you walk through this lesson several times and begin to engage your heart in the reality of these truths; you will begin to experience more freedom in your perceptions, in your thoughts, and in your heart. However, you will need to build these truths in your heart and life by studying and meditating. Eventually, your mind will begin to default toward a discovery mindset. A discovery mindset creates tremendous hope for each of us. You will come to realize that all you need to be successful and to win in life is readily available to you, simply by discovery. When I am sharing these truths with individuals and groups, I often say: "Life is easy. Life is not hard. What makes life appear to be difficult, is the way we feel." I will delve more into this concept when we get to our third lesson on the Law of Discipline.

Once again, I want to make this clear. There is nothing in life that was not discovered. Not one single person has invented anything, worked through the process of owning a business or even developed skills in any sport, which did not employ the Law of Discovery. We do not have to force life to work. Life is designed to work. What we have to do is, discover the laws that govern life and line up our hearts, our will, and behavior, to work with these laws, not against them.

Gravity is not struggling to work. The law of lift is not struggling to work. The law of cause and effect is not struggling to work. The sun rises every day in the east, without a single problem. If you look at weather patterns you will notice that they produce certain types of storms. Nature is a perfect example of how simply life works. The problem with mankind is our unwillingness to work for and to cooperate with, these laws.

Life is easy. Life is not hard, what makes life appear to be difficult is the way we feel.

The reason I say, "Life is easy. Life is not hard and what makes life difficult is the way we feel." is because you and I can do anything that we were designed to do, with maximum results and excellence, if we can get past the way we feel. We must manage our feelings, so they work for us and not against us. The reality is that mankind is his own worst enemy. It is said that we can experience around 64,000 thoughts a day. These thoughts are connected to emotions and personal feelings that we have. Many of the deep-seated feelings are often connected to our self-worth and self-esteem. You and I must continually remember that we will have things occur externally and internally that attempt to agitate and railroad our feelings and emotional state.

Thoughts on the Canvas of Love

All of us have wayward beliefs in our souls, which can limit us in one way or another. This is what makes it seem so difficult, for so many people. Emotions and feelings fluctuate throughout the course of a day. These out of control states, sometimes foster depression, anger, frustration, laziness and various other types of negative dispositions. All of our thoughts have feelings that partner with them; this is why I said you can intentionally change your state,

It is said that we individually can experience around 64,000 thoughts a day.

at any time, to work for you and not against you. Self-awareness is paramount. Being mindful of your emotional state can play a tremendous role in forming internal habits. These habits can assist you on your journey to fulfill your destiny.

As you see, if we can stabilize our emotions and approach life with the understanding that every necessity is readily available, we will come into great wisdom. This wisdom will solve problems and create solutions. This wisdom will cause financial increase and assist us in having fruitful relationships. This kind of wisdom is available but must be sought after and discovered. The challenge is that most of us are so governed by the way we feel that we never get past those obstacles. Our feelings block our progress. We will discuss this more when we talk about the Law of Discipline.

Recall earlier, I made a statement about Bill Gates and Steve Jobs; these people and others like them were broke but had a dream that they simply would not give up on.

They were dogged in their process of discovery. The same applies to other inventors and entrepreneurs, Thomas Edison, for example, had a discovery mindset. When asked about the 1,000 times he failed trying to create the light bulb, he said he did not fail. He said he had simply found 1,000 ways that did not work. Understand that Thomas Edison employed the Law of Discovery to reveal how to sustain light. In all of these examples, as we said earlier, when the student is ready the teacher will appear, and preparation always meets opportunity. Now let's take some time to challenge a way of thinking, as it relates to opportunity.

CHAPTER 6

Opportunities in Abundance

One day, a friend of mine approached me, regarding a personal challenge he was having. He was very frustrated with his current employment and explained how difficult it had been for him to prosper where he lived. I patiently listened as he said, "I am thinking about leaving Chicago because there are no opportunities for me here." I empathized with his situation. I understood how he could feel frustrated. He continued to give more reasons and examples of his predicament. I continued to listen without much comment. Eventually, the conversation shifted to other subjects. After a few minutes, he brought the subject of opportunities, back to my attention.

I believe he may have been a bit aggravated, by my silence. Finally, he asked me what I thought about his opportunity problem. I said, "Well, if you feel you have a divine appointment or assignment in another city, then I would encourage you to follow providence, but if you or anyone else thinks, that going to another city is going to resolve your opportunity issue, you are wrong." I explained that opportunity is not external. On the contrary, opportunity is internal. It is imperative, that we change our perception of life and how it works.

Listen carefully, if you grab a magazine listing the top ten cities for the best employment opportunities and you decide to move to one of those cities, what happens if in the next year, the growth stops, and the opportunities dry up? Now you have a situation where you have uprooted your entire life and moved to an unfamiliar city, following the next big wave and have nothing; all because you looked for opportunities externally. You can see the fallacy in this approach. Of course, there are more fruitful areas, in certain cities. I am not making light of that, but in reality, this kind of thinking is very dangerous and will never yield a life beyond mediocrity.

Opportunities exist internally, not externally.

Every idea, every invention, every billion-dollar company, and every skyscraper existed first, beyond what your eyes can see. That means it existed in the realm of thought and imagination before it was manifested naturally. What that tells me is, all opportunities exist internally and not externally. You see, following the next big wave won't solve anything. You will still take the same barren mind, negative thoughts and unstable emotions, to your next destination. You cannot escape from yourself.

What needs to happen is that you need to internally grow by planting good seeds into fertile ground, with positive thoughts and stable emotions. That way, you can discover your own unique design, instead of running around trying to get someone else to tell you how to live or waiting for them to hand you an opportunity. We must learn how to discipline ourselves. We must be willing to think and imagine, acknowledging the laws that govern life, with creativity and consistency. Anyone who thinks that leaving one location to go to another will automatically improve their life is misguided. You may find a new job and even find a new spouse, but as the Word of God says, *"As a man thinks in his heart, so is he."* (Proverbs 23:7)

The same external challenges faced in a new location will yield the same disappointing results if you have made no internal strides. You will find yourself back in the same unsatisfying situations that motivated you to move in the first place. All true change is internal, before it manifests externally. Life runs in cycles. Stop looking for opportunities externally. The Law of Discovery says there is an inheritance that can be discovered through thought and imagination: by seeking, knocking and asking, I will find the inheritance.

What I find interesting is that these laws have no respect of persons. I shared earlier that I am a person of faith, but these laws will even work for a person that does not believe there is a God. What I am trying to get you to comprehend is that there is a treasure of wisdom that dwells within the universe. It is waiting for someone to harvest it. We are making a huge mistake if we think abundance comes from an outside source. Personally, I believe God wants everyone to win in life and have abundance. Simply because He is the source of all that is good. However, what I am referring to now is the mindset that looks externally for answers and looks for others to resolve their issues and to make life work for them.

You see, everything has to be discovered. Think about the amount of energy, focus and concentration that is applied toward finding a lost key. You are completely and fully engaged in this quest. You spend a lot of time and a lot of effort tossing this and digging through that, trying to find the key. You are actively involved in doing everything you possibly can, to find the missing key. Well, that same discipline and dogged determination should be applied to you discovering who you are, what your gifts and talents are and what your life design is. Sadly, most people will not spend time to invest in themselves. Most people are just too doggone lazy to make this happen. The enemy of discovery is laziness and slothfulness. If you seek, you shall find, if you knock the door shall be opened, and if you ask, it shall be given. These all require us to be engaged in intentional activity, focus, concentration, consistency and discipline.

Now let's explore what is meant by a discovery mindset. The Word of God declares that we should, *"Guard our heart with all diligence for out of our heart flow the boundaries, limitations, or the results of our life."* (Proverbs 4:23) The heart, again, is the most potent part of your being. It is a sophisticated system designed to produce, what is desired. The heart works on automatic, so whatever is in it, will produce without the assistance of your conscious mind. So, whatever you introduce to your heart in abundance, will eventually trigger your heart to produce what was programmed.

Opportunities in Abundance

The gateway to the heart is the mind. As you spend time learning a subject, your heart begins to accept this as the new norm. Understanding this, we should take advantage of this reality, by sending the desired message to the heart. This is what I meant earlier when I said, as we practice correct thinking, eventually our heart will default to that way of thinking. When we understand fully that everything in life is discovered, we will intentionally program our heart to be actively engaged in a discovering mode. This is more effective than being very passive and reactive.

> The gateway to the heart is the mind. As you spend time learning a subject, your heart begins to accept this as the new norm.

You will no longer think, at a heart level that things work by force. You will be persuaded, in the process of time and by thinking correctly, begin to consistently get answers to problems and will discover wisdom beyond your wildest dreams. Now you are in business! Your heart is able to do its job by connecting a bridge to our Creator and the resources in the universe, so those resources can find their way into your conscious mind. Now once again, I personally believe, as a person of faith, the resources in the universe were set in motion by our intelligent creator and that they are readily available for any person that seeks to find.

Now let's explore how a discovery mindset works. Recall earlier, our discussion about Thomas Edison and the light bulb. It is reported that he was asked about the fact that he had failed 1,000 times in his quest to invent the light bulb. Thomas Edison replied, "I did not fail 1,000 times. I simply found 1,000 ways that did not work." Successful people commonly think this way. We can learn a lot from Edison's statement. A person's perception is their reality, regardless of what other people think about the thing or subject. The real question is, what are you thinking and perceiving about Edison's attempts? You see, to those with a failure consciousness, the predominant thought would be, "Wow, you failed all those times?!!" With this way of thinking, the person is treating failure as an enemy, while Thomas Edison invited failure as a friend. For him, it was simply a partner in the process.

Edison would have never been able to fulfill his objective, if he looked at life as being hard, having a failure consciousness and thinking from a perspective of force. Instead, he employed persistence, resilience and proper thinking, to slowly but surely discover the wisdom that would enable him to complete his task. Thomas Edison knew the answer was close and he understood the importance of employing this law through seeking, knocking and asking. A discovery mindset is not a mindset of lack. It is a mindset of abundance. It is an optimistic mindset that thrives on the fact that the answer will not be denied. I love this story because it truly exemplifies the way all great things come into manifestation. Disappointment tries its best to stop us from pursuing our goals. However, if we start changing our perspective on failure and are persuaded that all

> **A discovery mindset is not a mindset of lack. It is a mindset of abundance.**

the resources to fulfill our dreams are readily available and that there is no one holding us back from obtaining them, then we will patiently dig until we find all the pieces to the puzzle.

For over twenty years, as I shared previously, I worked in business. In the different positions I held, I had to get used to hearing the word "No." Now, "No" for some, can dredge up painful feelings of rejection, but for the successful business minded individual, being told "No" is a necessary and part of the process. I simply believed that I had to experience some "No's" to get to the "Yes" I was seeking. To be successful in sales and business I had to have a discovery mindset.

You can train your mind to think this way about every challenge in life. It will require persistent and intentional thinking, but it is worth it. I have seen this work countless times in my own personal life. This way of thinking enabled me to win several business awards. It has enabled me also to earn an above-average income. It has allowed me to meet people I wouldn't have met and afforded me opportunities that I would not have been normally exposed to.

The lifestyle of discovery is an adventure. It is an exciting daily journey, once you get your heart moving in this direction. Now, I want to make sure you understand that you will still experience mixed emotions and your feelings may not always line up with what you are seeking. You will not feel heaven every day and there will be times when you will be challenged by fear or thoughts of lack and inability. As you employ correct thinking, you will get to a place of being in control of your wayward emotions. You will be equipped to hold captive negative emotions and feelings long enough to prove them wrong. Eventually, you will be able to dissipate and weaken the influence negativity may have on your pursuit.

The single most important thing, you and I could do to fulfill our God-given dreams is to manage the way we feel, through proper intentional thinking. Employing thinking that opens the flood gates of opportunities and using the kind of thinking that has propelled our society to the modern progressive place, it is today, is intentional thinking. Yes, a discovery mindset is vital. This mindset clearly understands the resources are readily available. We simply have to stay the course. *"Seek and ye shall find, knock and the door shall be opened, ask and it shall be given."*

Notice, earlier I mentioned that a person with a discovery mindset will not be denied. Well, here is the reason why. The Law of Discovery declares there is an absolute outcome. The phrases seek, knock and ask all have absolute outcomes. It says, seek and you will find, it doesn't say seek and you might find. It says, knock and the door will be opened, it doesn't say knock and the door might be opened. It doesn't say ask and it might be given, it says ask and it shall be given. I want you to realize, this is the way life works. Listen, these are absolute outcomes. I just have to seek, knock and ask and stay the course, because on the other side of this activity are guaranteed results. Now, there are two necessary and powerful tools required to make the journey to discover success; intentional correct thinking and asking the correct questions. Both of these tools must be employed on a consistent basis, if you are going to develop a discovery mindset.

Let's talk a little about intentional thinking. Most people do not think, especially those who read the Word of God. They don't think, they simply read and quote what is written. Thinking is so important to becoming successful in life. One of my mentors says, if he could start his career over again, one thing he would do is teach people how to think properly.

There is a right way and a wrong way to think. People that live above mediocrity, think differently than people that lead an average or below-average life. It is incredible how just a slight adjustment in the way we think, can have a tremendous impact on our ability to discover. There is a huge difference between people thinking, "I can't afford this" versus "How can I afford it?" The words "I can't" automatically send a message to the heart to stop seeking and knocking. However, the power of creativity is released by adjusting the "I can't" to "How can I?" This slight change activates the heart to search for answers.

The thoughts we foster as habits, will eventually turn into actions. If you and I think incorrectly, we are literally sabotaging the process of discovering life's answers. The word sabotage is defined as any underhanded interference with production. Sabotage also means, to disable or cripple. With this added light, you can see that wrong thinking will cripple and disable the process of discovery.

I want to add another important piece, to this area of discovery. Please pay close attention. At the core of life, this is how everything works. In the universe; information, wisdom, new ideas, new inventions, etc. are already active, available and in motion. Your heart and mind have been designed to gravitate naturally toward discovering what already exists. Wrong thinking will manifest more of the negative things, which you already have. Correct thinking empowers discovery and allows access to new things and new possibilities. It is that simple.

As you can see, this has nothing to do with force or making something happen. It has everything to do with being in congruence with laws that allow us to access the invisible realm. This is where wisdom awaits.

Now as we continue, you may be saying, "I can see what you are saying, but how do I kick start this process?" or perhaps, "Kelvin, I think that is just a special gift for certain people." I assure you, it is not a gift that one individual has, it is simply the way life works.

There are three things I know through personal experience that I believe are necessary to start this process:

1. You must have a hunger to find your unique design.
2. You must change your thinking habits.
3. You must learn to ask yourself the correct questions.

Opportunities in Abundance

This will activate the process of discovery in your life. The reason I start with realizing your unique design is that when you find your sweet spot, where your gifts, talents, and passions are, these three things become your natural flow in life. Finding your unique design is paramount to coming into your prosperity.

Many times, people attempt to do things just to make money or to be successful. This is the wrong path to take in your journey. I believe everything in life has a definite purpose and every human being has a mission and purpose in life, which connects to their unique design. Remember, life is like a puzzle. You discover the full picture piece by piece, one step at a time. I think one of the most tragic realities of the human race today, is that a large percentage of people have no clue what gifts and talents they possess or what is their purpose in life. This is why so many people are frustrated with their life.

Life is like a puzzle. You discover the full picture piece by piece, one step at a time.

Over the years, I have been fortunate to discover my personal calling and mission in life. I can tell you, from first-hand experience that it is possible to work day after day and be joyful about your work. This happens when your work lines up with who you are and what you were made for. I can talk, teach and write about developing human potential and leadership from natural and spiritual points of view, forever and never get tired of it. Teaching comes naturally to me. I love to teach, train, activate and inspire people toward the fulfillment of their dreams.

I would like to encourage you to begin the process of self-discovery, right now, if you haven't already. If you are not sure of your purpose or mission in life or if you are just not clear on your individual design, one of the ways you can enhance clarity in these areas is by taking the time to pinpoint the things in life you really enjoy. This is a good time to find a quiet spot and maybe sit outdoors in nature or in a solitary room and write down all of things that you like to do while asking yourself those good solid coaching questions, as you did earlier.

During your brainstorming session, consider doing and answering the following: List the things you have been involved in since you were a child. Engage your imagination and let it run, without limitations. Examine what you find joy and delight in doing. Consider what motivates you. Write down things you would do for other people and about places you would go for personal fulfillment if money were not an issue. What are you passionate about? What do people ask your advice about? What do you naturally do well? What did you neglect pursing because you thought you couldn't make any money doing it? Spend lots of time in prayer and reflection.

> Engage your imagination and let it run, without limitations. Examine what you find joy and delight in doing.

I also encourage reading books covering all the subjects that interest you. These days, you can listen to digital books while driving, exercising, cooking or just relaxing at home. I think reading is powerful because it allows you to see other people's world views and encourages broader thinking. Reading exposes you to greater possibilities and stirs imagination and hope. When you really find your true design, it is amazing how your life's vision will

> When you realize your true design, it is amazing how your entire life's vision will change.

change. Do whatever you need to do, to expose yourself to truth and discovery.

Now I want to bring up something that is really important, if you intend to really make a dent in the area of self-discovery. I mentioned earlier that mankind fell from the origin of love. You must have a transformation, if you haven't already, in the area of self-love. I am not talking about self-centered living. In fact, in order to have true life, you must let go of self-centered living. In the Word of God, Jesus declares that one must deny themselves and follow him. This is not the annihilation of self nor is it a form of self-hatred. It is a self-love intertwined with the love of God. All things in life were designed by our Creator, to serve you. Your fulfillment is not in things, it is in God. However, you can never reach your full potential until you are renewed in your mind with proper thinking about yourself.

A positive sense of self, good self-esteem and self-worth is the starting point for self-discovery. It is amazing that in the Word of God, Jesus says that the goal of life can be summed up with this truth: Every human being is summoned to love the Lord with all their heart, soul, and strength and to love their neighbor as they do themselves.

The Word of God also declares that men are to love their wives as they do themselves. Based on this statement, the key to loving others is to love ourselves. Well isn't that remarkable?

I dislike religion, because religion is all about manmade rules and regulations. Life doesn't work exclusively by rules and regulations. In reality, life really works by the love of God. So, you must love yourself first, if you are to find your unique design. In fact, love will reveal light for the discovery of your unique design. Why? Well, because the Creator designed you to help Him. He certainly wants you to have clarity to know to how you were designed, in order for you to be effective in your assignments.

I dislike religion, because religion is all about manmade rules and regulations.

At this point in your reading, it should be evident, that life is really not as difficult as it appears to be. Once again, the most difficult area in our lives to manage is our emotions and feelings. I hope you can see that life really is all about discovery and that nothing has been brought into being in the past or the future, by force. It is all basically manifested through thought. It is absolutely the truth, that all things are discovered. Nothing at its root was created by men or women. All of the materials needed to bring your God-given goals and dreams to pass, are waiting on you to discover them. It is not your sole responsibility to put the pieces together. The Creator will help you. You must simply begin by acting on all those ideas that have been floating around in your mind, lying dormant. The truths about discovery will ease the pressure for you to perform out of force and fear. The aim should be to know, out of the economy of God. This will allow for the flow of effortless discovery, which will yield higher overall results.

Up to this point, we have discussed two great laws that I consider master keys to unlocking and fulfilling your God-given destiny. The Law of Desire is the catalyst for the entire process. The universe must receive a definite command, stemming from a passionate desire, in order to manufacture positive results. We next discussed the fact that all of life is about discovery. Nothing is created from scratch; neither is anything forced into fruition. All the resources for things imagined in the heart of mankind are simply waiting to be discovered. Now, it has been an absolute delight to share with you about these two great master keys but the next key we must discuss is the most important key. It is the Law of Discipline.

CHAPTER 7

The Law of Discipline

Discipline is said to be the most important ingredient to success and is the most crucial of all the laws we've discussed. The Law of Discipline brings everything you have desired and discovered together. The Law of Discipline embodies doing what needs to be done, regardless of how you feel. It is the ability to do the right things and the most important things, consistently. Make no mistake, the other laws are important. You must desire with passion and know what you want, and you must employ the Laws of Discovery. However, without the Law of Discipline, you will never maximize your potential.

In studying the subjects of human behavior and personal development, there is consistent agreement amongst experts that self-discipline is the master key to the Laws of Achievement. The Law of Discipline is activated with the Law of Desire and the Law of Discovery. In fact, without discipline these other laws would be impotent. It is through discipline that desire, and discovery rise to their place of influence on your journey towards your God given destiny. Once again, remember that laws govern everything that happens on our planet and everything flows in cycles. There is a mid-phase in all manifestation. The mid-phase is the unseen growth phase that can't be grasped by natural senses. It is where mankind engages in battle.

Now we really don't have a problem, for the most part, comprehending that what we sow, we reap. Since thoughts and words are like seeds, it is easy to understand that process. It is the mid-phase that brings us our greatest challenge. After the sowing of the seed, we must have the discipline to wait for growth. The Law of Discipline must be employed daily. Enacting the most important priorities, during the time when it appears that nothing is happening.

A great illustration of this is what we see when a farmer plants seeds and daily waters and cultivates the fields. It is necessary to have light and water consistently to ensure a good harvest. On the surface, it looks like nothing is happening. For days and days, it looks this way, yet the farmer remains consistent in employing all of his agricultural skills and wisdom necessary to ensure he yields a harvest.

You are the farmer and your life is the field. Like the farmer in a natural field there are things you must be disciplined to do every day, while God does his part to send the rain, sun, and oxygen required to grow the crops. The miracle of being fruitful only happens when someone with discipline, tills the ground and consistently cultivates it. Farmers participate proactively, with the laws that govern farming. Likewise, we must develop the discipline to activate and apply all that we receive, once the Law of Desire and the Law of Discovery have done their job.

If discipline is a rule or system that governs conduct or activity and if it is, indeed, an order or prescribed conduct or a pattern of behavior; <u>then all people are disciplined.</u>

Discipline can be defined as the rules or systems that govern conduct or activity. It is an orderly or prescribed conduct or pattern of behavior. In the past, I have taught people whom I once considered to be undisciplined in life. I thought they failed to achieve their desired goals and objectives, because they had no self-discipline.

Over the past few years, I have come into a higher level of awareness. What I have come to discover can be seen in the definition of discipline itself. If discipline is a rule or system that governs conduct or activity and if it is, indeed, an order or prescribed conduct or a pattern of behavior, then all people are disciplined. Your mode of discipline is either working for you or against you, but you are disciplined. You are disciplined in being lazy or you are disciplined in procrastinating or being inconsistent.

Discipline is a pendulum that swings both ways. It is simply the pattern of behavior that you have chosen or allowed to be activated and employed in your life every day. You see, you and I are either consistently disciplined to do the right things or the wrong things. Regardless, in the process of time, we will have what we've ordered in our lives. This perspective should help you see that you always have some pattern of discipline working in your life. The key is to begin to be intentional, in the guidance and activation of these patterns. Make them work for you, to achieve the God given goals and dreams you are responsible for birthing into the earth realm.

There are no excuses. We must stop playing the blame game and come to grips with the fact that we are responsibilities. Each of us is responsible for leaving this planet better than when we came into it. We should positively impact the world around us and bear good fruit. For so many of us, the Law of Discipline is working in a negative mode, yielding only barrenness and fruitlessness. It is time to act. It is time to change our daily living patterns. We must understand that everything we do each day, is either being governed by our feelings and emotions or they are intentionally being governed by personal commands or choices. Like it or not, that is the truth.

I want you to think about your life and the great gift you have been given to be able to govern and guide your life. The gift I am speaking of is the gift of volition. It is the ability to choose the direction your life takes. You must accept full responsibility. God doesn't control your will. The past does not have the right to control your will or choices. Other human beings definitely do not have the power or the right to choose for you. To make the Law of Discipline our friend, we must intentionally employ it and tell it what to govern. The art of planning is a friend of discipline.

CHAPTER 8

Planning: Discipline's Power Twin

Now earlier, if you recall, I shared this amazing quote that came from a discussion I had with an associate of mine. The gift of imagination allows us to be where we are going before we get there. This is powerful. Stephen Covey said in his book, *The Seven Habits of Highly Effective People*, that we all ought to begin with the end in mind. This is absolutely the truth. It is a truth that was instituted by the Creator, before the beginning of time. Think about it, in your mind's eye, you can see the finished product, objective or goal prior to its manifestation. This is remarkable. Well, since we can see the end, we can and should govern our lives with the daily disciplines that will transport us, to our expected end. So, in order to have the Law of Discipline work in our lives, we must have a plan.

As you know by now, I like to define words and phrases to make sure we are on the same page. So, listen again, closely. The definition of a plan is a detailed program; a method for achieving an end; a set of actions that have been thought through to achieve something. A plan is an intentionally written blueprint of a desired outcome. Other words that are synonymous with plan are arrangement, design, game plan, road map, system, and strategy. Notice that all of these are orderly and prescribed. Also, they all imply a definite pattern. Discipline is the software that we run our intentional preplanned program, strategy, road map, or design on.

> **There is a masterpiece awaiting our command. We simply need to take action.**

This is incredible! We actually have the power and ability to dictate our future by planning. We can plug our plans into compatible goals with an orderly pattern of behavior that will assist in accomplishing a desired outcome. Eureka! There is a masterpiece awaiting our command. We simply need to take action. Now, as you recall, another truth I have realized and shared is the fact that life was not designed by the Creator to be difficult. In fact, from a governance perspective, the earth runs in a smooth orderly fashion. So, the perspective I have on life that I teach in my "Mastermind seminars," is that "Life is not hard. Life is easy. What really makes life difficult is the way you feel."

Most people can follow directions, so let's complete a brief exercise. Clap your hands. Turn your head left, then right. Now blink your eyes. Ok, sniff. Count to 10. Now exhale. Now inhale. Did you struggle to follow my instructions? No, you didn't. So, that rules out the excuse that we can't respond properly to instructions. So, if it's that easy why we won't just follow the instructions to win in life. It's very simple. Remember, I mentioned that we have no problem understanding the law of cause and effect and that our greatest challenge is during the mid-phase, the growing season. This is what I was referring to. Once the desired outcome is discovered in seed form, emotions and feelings strive daily, to gain governance over good plans and to abort and sabotage the strategy before it has a chance to take root.

BEWARE: Once the desired outcome is discovered in seed form, emotions and feelings compete daily to gain governance over good plans, urging you to abort and sabotage the strategy, before it has a chance to take root.

You see, a lot of us have started with the right idea and with good intentions but fail in the area of follow through. Instead of following a prescribed consistent program that will steer us toward our goals, we are more disciplined to act based on the way we feel. These actions do not bring us closer to realizing our dreams.

In order to accomplish the God given goals and dreams in life, faith must be activated daily. This faith must declare that regardless of how I feel and no matter what my current circumstances appear to be, my plan will lead me to my desired outcome. The sails must be set in the direction of the desired outcome. The details and sacrifices must be mapped out, in order to get there. We must trust the plan and work it every day.

Now, we could be passive and just allow things to happen. We could employ a daily dependence on how we feel to steer our actions and allow the external forces of life to dictate the path we should take, or we can choose to rebel

> The Law of Discipline is all about commanding our life through a plan; to go in the direction of our intentional design on a daily basis, regardless of how we feel.

against the instability of our emotions and feelings. We could willfully and deliberately take charge of our state and command our life to follow a daily prescribed path. The latter is what the Law of Discipline is all about. It is commanding our life through a plan. It is to actually go in the direction of our intentional design, regardless of how we feel. It is the power to daily accomplish all the important parts of the plan, especially when we do not feel like it.

CHAPTER 9

The Myth of the Gift of Discipline

Now let's talk about planning. I have accomplished quite a bit in life but, like all people, I struggle with discipline. It is remarkable how this works. Over the years, I have invested in studying the most accomplished people of our time. I have discovered that we all share an incredible, common challenge. It is the daily struggle to employ the Law of Discipline. For some strange reason, I believed there was some kind of magic power or deep revelation that enabled people to act with unwavering discipline. Well, this is simply not true. From all-star athletes to business professionals and entrepreneurs, from pastors and entertainers to those with great leadership legacies, this common truth exists. No one *FEELS* like doing the right and important things, each day they awaken.

The only difference between us and the people who have achieved through staunch discipline is that these people **decided** to continue to press, regardless of how they felt or what their daily obstacles were. Achievers learn to live intentionally. I was encouraged to hear how many mornings some of the best of the best have been tempted to stay in bed a little longer or how they were tempted to chat at the water cooler when there was work to be done. Every now and then, even achievers want to eat the wrong thing or play a little while longer. They would love to live spontaneously, without a plan, as well. There are days they would rather not sacrifice and actually take a few shortcuts. However, these people without exception had or have a sense of what it really takes to be above average. Now, like I mentioned, while talking about the Law of Discovery, when you find your life's design there seems to be an empowerment that follows. I want to make sure you realize that regardless of even finding your sweet spot, so to speak, we will continue to have daily yearnings to follow our feelings.

Our edge is found in daily, deliberate planning.

This is why planning is absolutely vital, if we are going to achieve in life. Without a plan you really do plan to fail. You see, without a written plan you are left vulnerable to contrary thoughts and emotions that will derail your progress. Earlier, I mentioned that you and I can have approximately 64,000 thoughts per day. We also have the accompanying emotions and feelings, to go along with those thoughts. The mere fact that our soul is experiencing all of this activity daily tells me that we must have some way of anchoring life with intention. There is too much going on, so we have to give our plans an edge. Our edge is found in daily, deliberate planning and execution.

The Myth of the Gift of Discipline

Now, I want you to know I have not arrived in this area of discipline. I am, however happy to report, that I have left the runway. You see, it is without question, nearly impossible to win this daily fight without a road map. One of my Mentors, John Maxwell, shared with our team that every day he writes and when he says every day, he means every day. When he feels good, he writes and when he is not feeling good, he writes. Why? Because he has a prescribed daily plan. This discipline has enabled John Maxwell to become a best-selling author and to release one great book, after another. Now, like most people, we feel that we are not free within the parameters of such structure. Well, this is the furthest thing from the truth.

In reality, the more thought you give to your plan, the more important things you will find to prioritize and inject into your plan and the more you will accomplish in your life on a daily basis. You will find that you will experience more freedom by developing a daily plan and activating discipline, in every area of your life. You will be able to accomplish and experience things that you didn't think were ever possible. Yes, discipline is the master key to achievement but without a daily plan, you will not have the fuel you need to make the journey.

Most people dislike the idea of having a written plan. They find it suffocating and restrictive. I personally, in the past, have rebelled against this same regimen. In fact, I kept thinking I was the exception and that I could be highly productive without this discipline. Well, I am here to tell you, I am now a believer in this daily necessity. I must have a daily road map, or plan, that I follow.

There are several benefits to have a prescribed plan. One is that a daily plan can help you stay focused. It also allows you work on the important and not always just react to the urgent. The execution of a daily plan also encourages the development of one's self-esteem. It is a proven fact that each time you accomplish something, your self-confidence and self-worth increases. This reality gives rise to higher future productivity and creativity. It also fuels our energy to stay on the intentional path which we have personally designed. Having a daily plan can give rise to a phenomenal work ethic, which breeds continuous self-improvement and productivity. In my opinion, planning is essential in assisting us in acquiring the accurate disciplines needed, in order to reach our desired destination.

The linchpin to discipline is choice.

Now, the linchpin to discipline is choice. However, this choice should not be predominately influenced by how we feel or swayed by our emotions. If you have a definite aim in life you will be passionate about it. Your desire will be red hot for the intended outcome. You will increase your odds of success by choosing correctly, each day. There is so much more to be said on this subject, that is not covered in this reading, but I would encourage you to study along these lines.

Another advantage of planning and actually programming the plan into your discipline is that it allows for incredible opportunity to employ the mind, heart and imagination. Once again, most people are not intentional about thinking. We all need to activate our minds toward proactive thinking. Now, this will take discipline, but thinking with intention will lower the bridge and allow for the crossing over of ideas from the Creator, directly to our hearts. It will open up the flood gates for discovery allowing our daily plans to have more clarity and for us to consistently make adjustments. We chart our daily course. In the Word of God, much is written about the importance of right thinking. In fact, one of the poetic books called, The Psalms, encourages meditation and gift wraps the promise of prosperity for the disciplined thinker and executer.

CHAPTER 10

The Benefits of Disciplined Life

There are so many great things that are birthed out of the Law of Discipline. The benefits are countless. They range from having a healthy physical body with lots of energy to having strong fulfilled Godly relationships. They encompass the ability to save money and to invest wisely. They help you to learn to appreciate and to delay immediate gratification, all of which are fruits of discipline. The Law of Discipline will also set you apart from mediocrity. It will enable you to connect and engage with people on higher levels in life.

Please understand I am not implying that people who are wealthy or who hold high social status are automatically better or deserving of more admiration than anyone else. I am not simply esteeming status or position. What I am saying is our heart is always seeking greater expression and growth and at new levels of awareness we can realize more of our potential if we surround ourselves with successful people who are like-minded. Disciplined successful people can offer personal insights, to inspire your advancement in productivity and maximize your potential. Therefore, you will come to realize the need to connect with more skilled, able men and women. They can serve you in developing your path, in order to add value to more people.

You see, it's an incredible cycle of love and abundance that is activated when this law is in motion. Without employing the Law of Discipline, your life becomes victim to entropy, chaos, disorder, degradation, and randomness. In other words, your life begins, in essence, to rust away.

How many people have already gone to the grave without giving rise to their God-given potential and talents?

How many people have already gone to the grave without giving rise to their God-given potential and talents? What does the Creator desire to manifest, for His glory, in your life? How does He want to use you, to add value to someone else's life? Could it be that our lack of accurate discipline is preventing this added value? This is real talk. Whether you agree with this fact or not, every ethnicity and group of people on this earth are yearning for the greatness that lies dormant, in each of our lives.

We were born in this time, to make some kind of positive contribution to humanity. We must resist taking the path of least resistance and begin to train ourselves to follow the divine path; the path toward the way life should be. Each day, we must choose to be proactive about life. We must change the way we think about life and we must resist negativity, excuses and blaming others. It is time for each of us to abandon a passively disciplined life that is governed by false feelings, born of low self-esteem and limiting beliefs. This unwanted birth desires to rob us and to sabotage our journey toward higher achievement. Instead, give rise to the higher calling of love, to discover the great power and blessing that comes from an intentionally disciplined life. There is an abundant supply for you in the areas of desire, discovery and discipline.

CHAPTER 11

The Law of Meditation

It is significant that I discuss one of the most misunderstood life changing concepts that is continuously referred to in the Word of God. Unfortunately, the gospel message in the Western world has embraced the Greek philosophical ideal that knowledge is king. Our churches in the United States have become incubators for knowledge accumulation. We have embraced, for the most part that the accumulation of knowledge is what changes our lives. It is amazing how many scholars live defeated lives and we see very little life transformation in the lives of parishioners throughout the world. Why is this? It's simple. Life change does not happen at the mental level; mentally agreeing that the Word of God is true will NOT change us. I submit to you and every other Christ-follower that the missing link to transformation is employing of the law of meditation. I have much to say about this important discipline but will only touch upon it in this writing.

What is remarkable to me is the fact that this law is mentioned as a continuous thread in the Word of God. There will be, at best, what is called behavior modification when we go the way of the Western world with knowledge accumulation. In order to see life change, the Word and the follower must become one flesh. This ONLY happens when the heart engages and embraces truth. Meditation is the tool that God gave mankind to engage the heart at an intimate level with Him. The employment of meditation, in active heart work is what will allow these three laws to effortlessly manifest. I am reminded of the quote from Psalms 1:1-3,

> *¹Blessed is the man that walketh not in the counsel of the ungodly, nor stands in the way of sinners, nor sits in the seat of the scornful; ²but his delight is in the law of the Lord; and in his law doth he meditate day and night.* [at the end of this Psalm is the result of following this instruction.] *³And he shall be like a tree planted by the rivers of water, that bringeth forth his fruit in his season; his leaf also shall not wither; and whatsoever he doeth shall prosper.*

It is clear and it is obvious, my Lord, how we have missed it in a big way, but it's time to recover this truth and not allow this tool to be misused by eastern religions, mystics and the occult. Clearly the Psalms declares blessing and prosperity to the man that engages in meditating the laws, commands, statues of the Word of God.

Desire grows immensely and destiny is discovered swiftly when we choose the Lord's way of meditation. I admonish you to study the subject from a biblical perspective and to form the discipline of constantly engaging your heart with God in meditation and I guarantee your life will never be the same. As a believer, you will live in an incredible awareness of the Father's love and you will no longer live under the burden of rules and regulations trying to get your life to work, now to this, I must say AMEN.

As your humble tour guide, we have taken a trip of learning, sharing and realization, through this book. Unfortunately, this signals the end of our time together, for now. Do not fret; I have great news for you! I have imparted to you, the knowledge and strategies I have been given. This will serve as a catalyst for your next, higher level of living. I pass on to you, your ticket to continue on to your next destination. Our Creator will continue to guide you into deeper waters. Do not fear! Just ahead, is great light to illuminate the depth of wisdom and riches He has availed to you. Choose the path you will take in the days to come. Be patient and invite continuous improvement and humility, to be your frequent guest. In fact, make the decision to build a room for the two of them to abide.

I salute you my friend, bon voyage! Onward to greater discoveries! May your future be full of joy and victory as you continue on your journey. Activate your desire and become clear about what you want. Seek and you shall find, knock and the door shall be opened, ask and it shall be given, for this is the Law of Discovery, that has opened its arms wide to you. Remember, you can win in every area of your life. From the Creator's perspective, "Life is not hard. Life is easy. What makes life seem so difficult is the way we feel." The key to curing emotional inconsistency is to activate and employ the Law of Discipline. Now again, be patient. It won't happen overnight. If you work at it daily, you will watch your ship set sail on the winning ocean of life. There it is my friend, Success in 3D.

Kelvin Easter is Founder and Senior Leader of Destined to Win Christian Center located in Park Forest, IL. Kelvin has a grace to build Christ in God's people through revelatory, simplistic and relevant teaching and preaching. He has a passion to raise up leaders through four generations and has an assignment to restore the male seed. Kelvin and his wife Tonya have two adult children, Isaiah and Chanel. They reside in South Holland, Illinois.

Pastor Kelvin's educational background includes a Bachelor of Arts from Columbia College. He is an alumnus of the Jack Hayford School of Pastoral Nurture and has started working towards his master's degree in Divinity at The King's University in Van Nuys, California. He was employed for twenty years with DeVry University. Kelvin worked the last eight years of his twenty-year tenure as the Senior Director of Admissions for DeVry's Chicago Campus. He is certified as a Ministry Coach through Ministry Coaching International and is a Certified coach, speaker and trainer through the John Maxwell

Team. Kelvin is the President of Leading-Edge Legacy, a personal and leadership development company. Also, he is the Founder of "TransforMEN", a male development ministry for the 21st century.

Follow Kelvin Easter on Facebook at: https://www.facebook.com/kelvin.easter.9